The Nile River

Major Rivers of the World Series Grade 4 |
Children's Geography & Cultures Books

BABY PROFESSOR
EDUCATION KIDS

First Edition, 2019

Published in the United States by Speedy Publishing LLC, 40 E Main Street, Newark, Delaware 19711 USA.

© 2019 Baby Professor Books, an imprint of Speedy Publishing LLC

Baby Professor Books are available at special discounts when purchased in bulk for industrial and sales-promotional use. For details contact our Special Sales Team at Speedy Publishing LLC, 40 E Main Street, Newark, Delaware 19711 USA. Telephone (888) 248-4521 Fax: (210) 519-4043.

10 9 8 7 6 * 5 4 3 2 1

Print Edition: 9781541953659
Digital Edition: 9781541956650

See the world in pictures. Build your knowledge in style.
www.speedypublishing.com

Contents

The River Nile in Egypt

The Nile River is the longest river in the world! In this book, you will learn all about the Nile, its climate, plants, animals, and people. Let's take a trip down the Nile!

The Backwards River

The Nile River is sometimes called the "Backwards River" because it flows from south to north

The Nile River is 4,132 miles (6649.8 kilometers) long. That makes it the longest river in the world! Most rivers flow from north to south but the Nile flows from south to north. This is why it is sometimes called the Backwards River.

The Nile is located in northeastern Africa. It starts south of the equator and flows north. It runs through rainforest, grassland, and even the Sahara desert. The Nile flows through parts of 10 different countries. It ends in Egypt where it empties out into the Mediterranean Sea.

MEDITERRANEAN SEA

NILE

SINAI

CIARO

GIZA

ISRAEL

WESTERN DESERT

SHARM EL SHEIKH

HURGADA

LIBYA

EGYPT

RED SEA

LUXOR

The Nile River ends in Egypt where it empties out into the Mediterranean Sea

SUDAN

11

Three rivers feed the Nile. They are the White Nile, the Blue Nile, and the Atabara. The Blue Nile is the longest of the three rivers. It is 907 miles (1459.6

Blue Nile River in Bahir Dar, Ethiopia

kilometers) long. The White Nile is around 500 miles (804.6 kilometers). The Atabara is also about 500 miles (804.6 kilometers) long.

White Nile River in Murchison Falls National Park, Uganda, East Africa

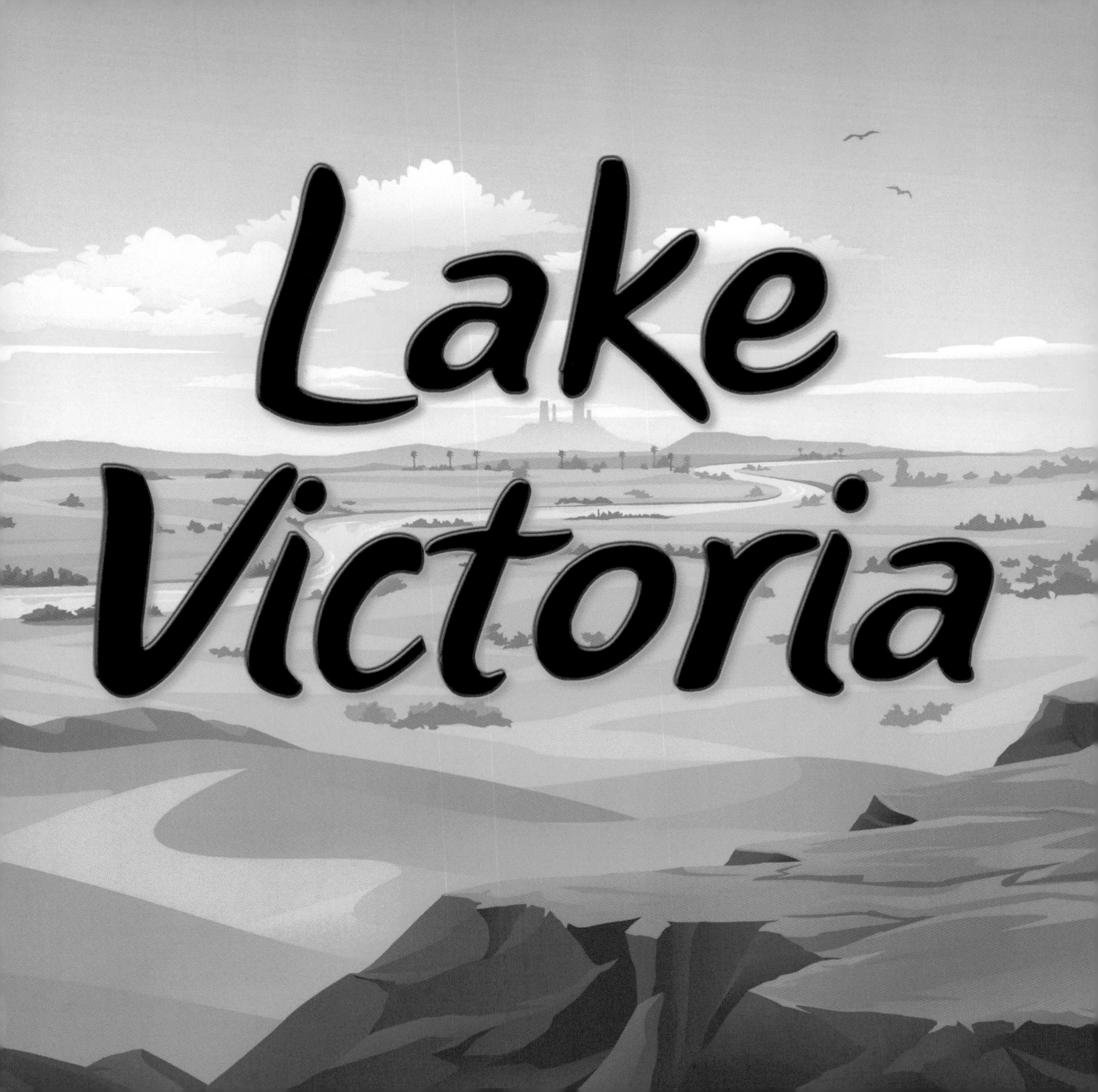
Lake
Victoria

Map of Lake Victoria

Lake Victoria is the biggest reservoir of water for the Nile. It keeps the river flowing all year. Lake Victoria is the largest lake in Africa! It covers an area of 26,828 square miles (69,484.2 square kilometers). The lake is 210 miles (337.9 kilometers) at its widest from north to south and 150 miles (241.4 kilometers) from east to west. Its coastline is over 2,000 miles (3218.6 kilometers) long. The deepest part of the lake is 270 feet (82.2 meters) deep. Lake Superior is the only freshwater lake that is bigger.

Lake Victoria is bordered by Tanzania, Uganda, and Kenya. The lake is home to over 200 species of fish. This makes fishing an important part of life on the lake. Lake Victoria is one of the most densely populated areas in Africa. There are many inhabited islands.

Fishing is an important part of life on Lake Victoria

Queen Victoria

The lake was originally called Ukerewe by the locals. The first European to ever see the lake was an explorer named John Hanning Speke, in 1858. He named the lake after Queen Victoria.

John Hanning Speke

The Nile River Basin and Delta

The following labels appear on the map:

Mediterranean Sea

JORDAN
PALESTINE
ISRAEL
IRAQ

Suez Canal

Cairo

SAUDI ARABIA

LIBYA

EGYPT

Aswan

Lake Nasser

HALAIB

CHAD

Kajbar

Merowe

Dagash

Shereik

Red Sea

Atbarah

SUDAN

Khartoum

Khashm al-Girba

ERITREA

Asmara

Jebel Aulia

AL-JAZIRAH

Tekeze

Nile Basin

White Nile

Blue Nile

Sennar

Lake Tana

Roseires

Tana Beles

Renaissance

ETHIOPIA

Sabat

Addis Ababa

CENTRAL AFRICAN REPUBLIC

SOUTH SUDAN

Gibe III

Lake Abaya

Juba

DEMOCRATIC REPUBLIC OF THE CONGO

UGANDA

Lake Kyoga

Lake Turkana

Owen Falls

Kampala

KENYA

Major dams
☗ operational
☗ under planning

Lake Victoria

Nairobi

RWANDA

0   250   500 km

BURUNDI   TANZANIA

The Nile River Basin covers about 10 percent of the African continent. It is bordered by the Mediterranean Sea in the north. The Red Sea Hills and the Ethiopian Plateau are to the west. Lake Victoria and the East African Highlands are south of the river basin. The Libyan Desert and the Marrah Mountains border it on the east.

The Nile River Basin covers about 10% of the African continent

MEDITERRANEAN SEA

NILE DELTA

EGYPT

NILE RIVER

GULF OF SUEZ

The Nile River Delta is in northern Egypt. When a river meets the ocean, it spreads out into a triangle shape called a delta. The Nile dumps a lot of silt here before flowing into the sea. Mud made of clay, rocks, soil, and nutrients left behind by a river is called silt.

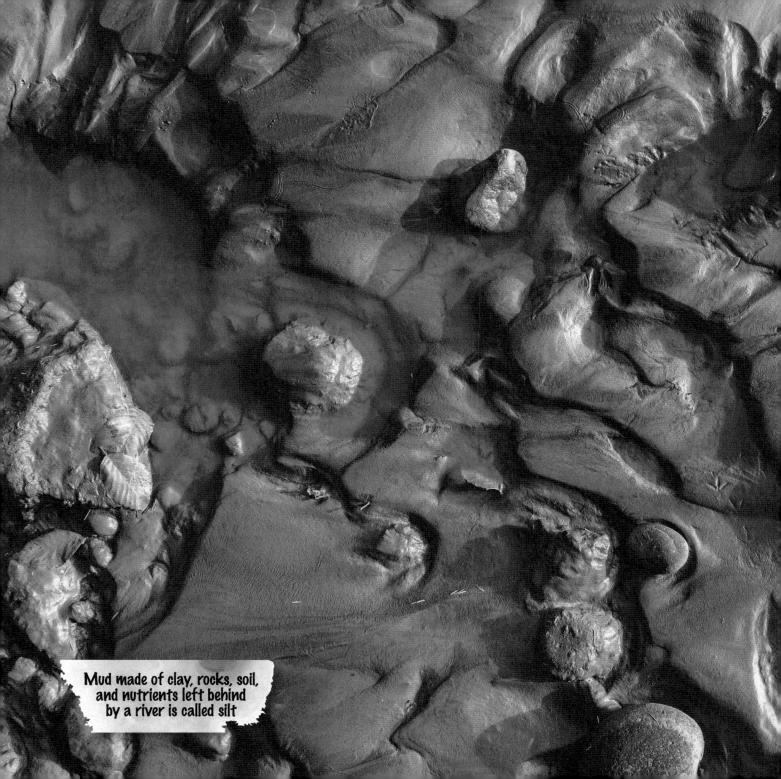

Mud made of clay, rocks, soil, and nutrients left behind by a river is called silt

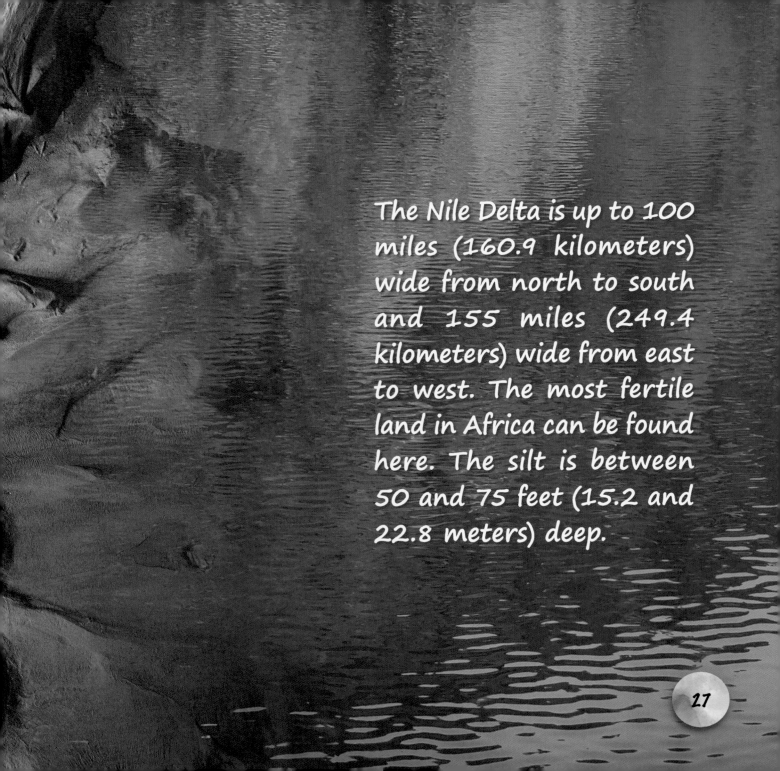

The Nile Delta is up to 100 miles (160.9 kilometers) wide from north to south and 155 miles (249.4 kilometers) wide from east to west. The most fertile land in Africa can be found here. The silt is between 50 and 75 feet (15.2 and 22.8 meters) deep.

The area around the Nile River was called "Black Land" because the rich silt left behind by the river was black

The name Nile comes from a Greek word meaning river valley. The area around the Nile has an older name though. It was originally

called Kem, Kemi, or Kemet. It means black or Black Land. It was called this because the rich silt left behind by the river was black.

Climate on the Nile

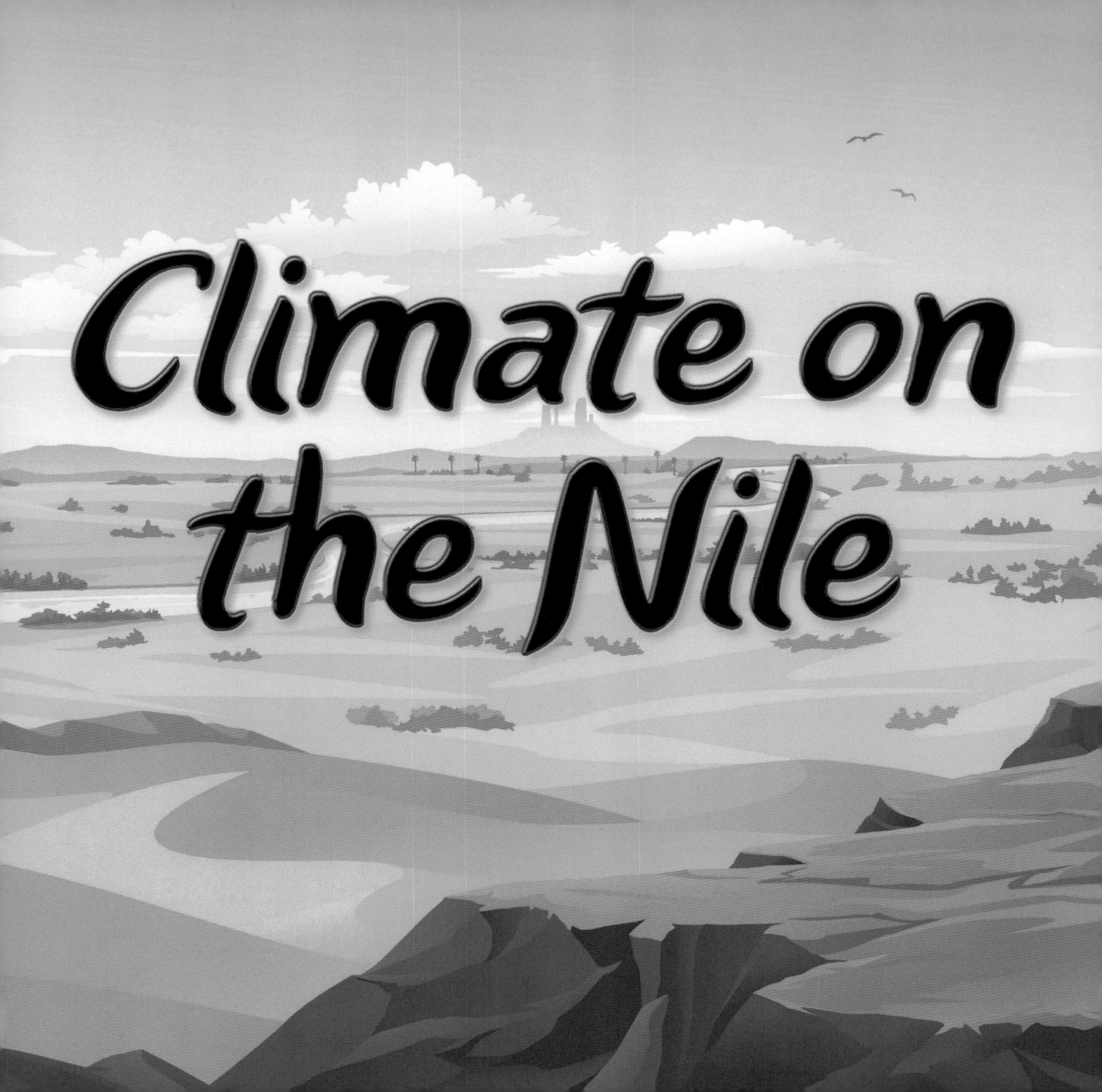

There are rainforests
along the Nile

The climate varies from place to place along the Nile. There are rainforests, swamps, grasslands, mountains, highlands, and deserts. Some places get up to 60 inches (152.4 centimeters) of rain in winter. Other places get no rain at all during the same time.

In tropical areas to the south, the temperature stays between 60 and 80° Fahrenheit (15.5° and 26.6° Celsius). In the desert, near the middle of the Nile, it can get up to 105° Fahrenheit (40.5° Celsius). It can sometimes get up to 117° Fahrenheit (47.2° Celsius) in the north.

A view of the Nile River in Cairo, Egypt

Cairo, the capital of Egypt, is near the Nile Delta and the Mediterranean Sea. There, the temperature stays around 70° Fahrenheit (21.1° Celsius) in winter.

Yearly Flood

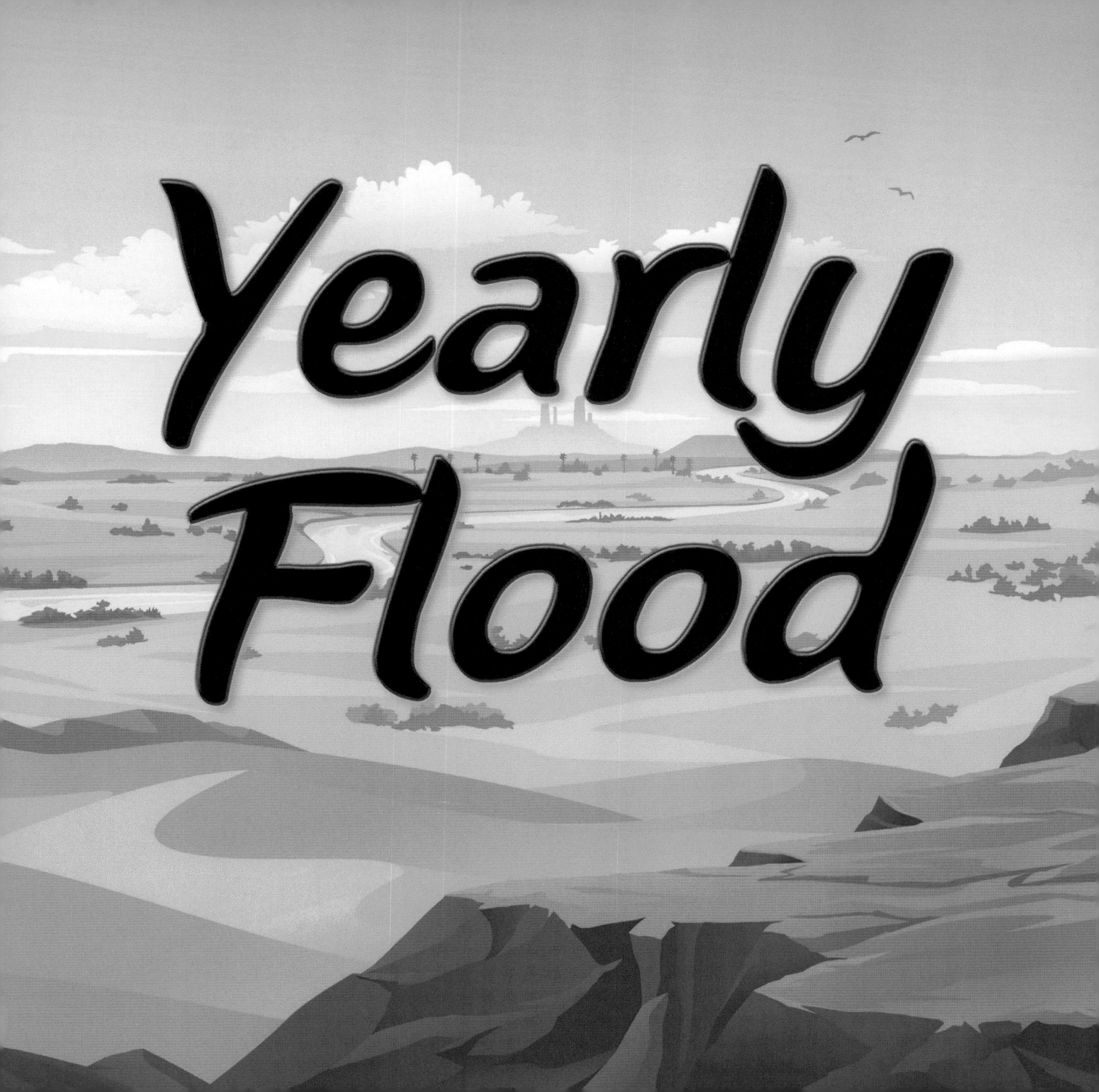

The Nile floods every year. The flood leaves behind silt. The silt makes farming possible in the desert.

Heavy rains upstream in Ethiopia and South Sudan cause the water to rise in summer. The Nile reaches its highest level near the middle of September. In November and December, the water level drops quickly. The river is at its lowest between March and May.

The Nile River floods every year

Plants and Animals

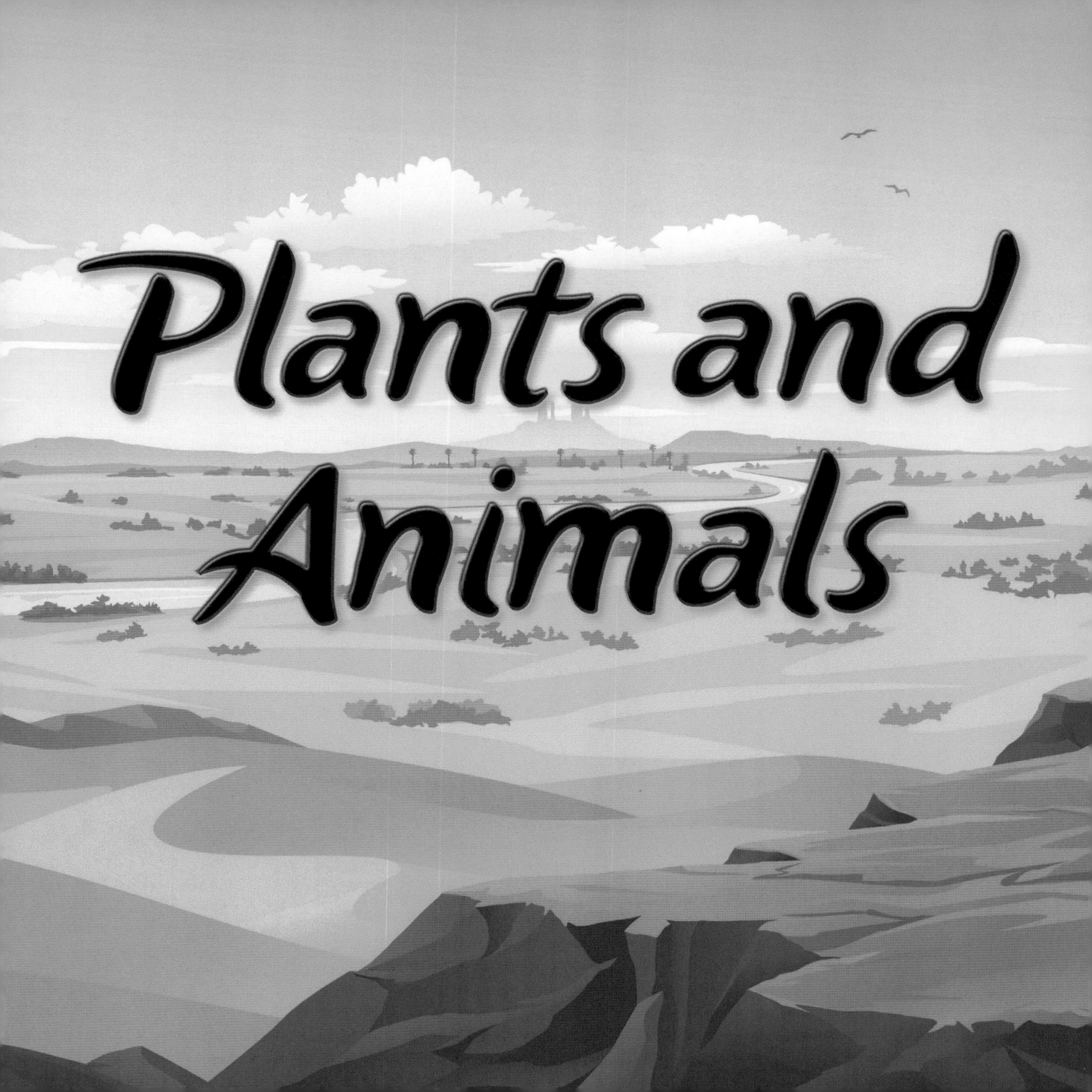

The Nile River stretches across different landscapes

*D*ifferent landscapes have different types of plants and animals. The Nile River stretches across rainforests, plains, deserts, and swamps.

In the tropical rainforests around the southern Nile, there are banana trees, rubber trees, bamboo, ebony trees, and coffee growing.

Banana trees

In the plains of Sudan, there are grasslands, sparse bushes, and thorny trees.

Nile River near Sesebi, Sudan

Cattails

In swampy areas, there are papyrus, cattails, water lettuce, water hyacinth, and tall grass similar to bamboo. Over 100 types of grass grow along the Nile River bank.

Papyrus is an important plant. Before paper was invented, people wove strips of papyrus together into long sheets. Once the sheets were pressed and dried, they could be drawn or written on. Many papyrus scrolls exist today that are thousands of years old!

Papyrus

The Nile is home to many interesting animals. Tilapia, catfish, tigerfish, and eels are some of the Nile's fish.

Tigerfish

Eels

Catfish

Tilapia

The Nile Perch is a fish that can grow to be 6 feet (1.8 meters) long and weigh 300 pounds (136 kilograms)!

Softshell turtles, monitors lizards, and many species of snakes also live in the Nile.

Snake

Monitor lizard

Softshell turtle

Some Nile animals are very dangerous. The Nile Crocodile can grow to be 20 feet (6 meters) long and weigh 2,200 pounds (997.9 kilograms)!

Nile crocodiles

Hippopotamuses can get up to 11.5 feet (3.5 meters) long, 5 feet (1.5 meters) tall, and weigh 7,000 pounds (3175.1 kilograms)! Their skin can be 2 inches (5 centimeters) thick in places, and their bottom canine teeth can grow to 12 inches (30.4 centimeters)!

Hippopotamuses

Farming and Irrigation

Farmland along the Nile River

People living near the Nile include Arabs and many African tribes. Most of these people make a living by farming. Farming in the desert can be tricky though.

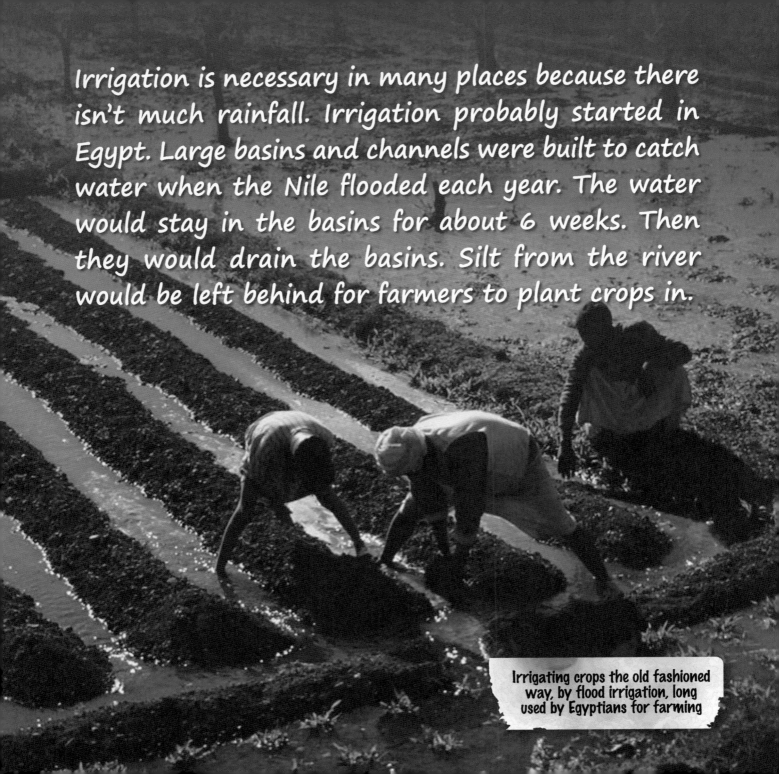

Irrigation is necessary in many places because there isn't much rainfall. Irrigation probably started in Egypt. Large basins and channels were built to catch water when the Nile flooded each year. The water would stay in the basins for about 6 weeks. Then they would drain the basins. Silt from the river would be left behind for farmers to plant crops in.

Irrigating crops the old fashioned way, by flood irrigation, long used by Egyptians for farming

Today, dams are used to hold and direct water. Farmers can get water to irrigate crops all year-round because of the dams. Dams also provide hydroelectric power.

The Aswan High Dam, is an embankment dam built across the Nile in Aswan, Egypt, between 1960 and 1970

Farmers grow a variety of crops around the Nile. Wheat is the most important but millet, rice, and corn are some other grains that are grown.

Wheat

Some other crops are beans, garlic, and onions. Figs, pomegranates, dates, and grapes are some fruits.

Garlic and onion

Cotton and flax are also grown.
Both can be used to make clothing.

Flax

Cotton

Ancient Kingdoms

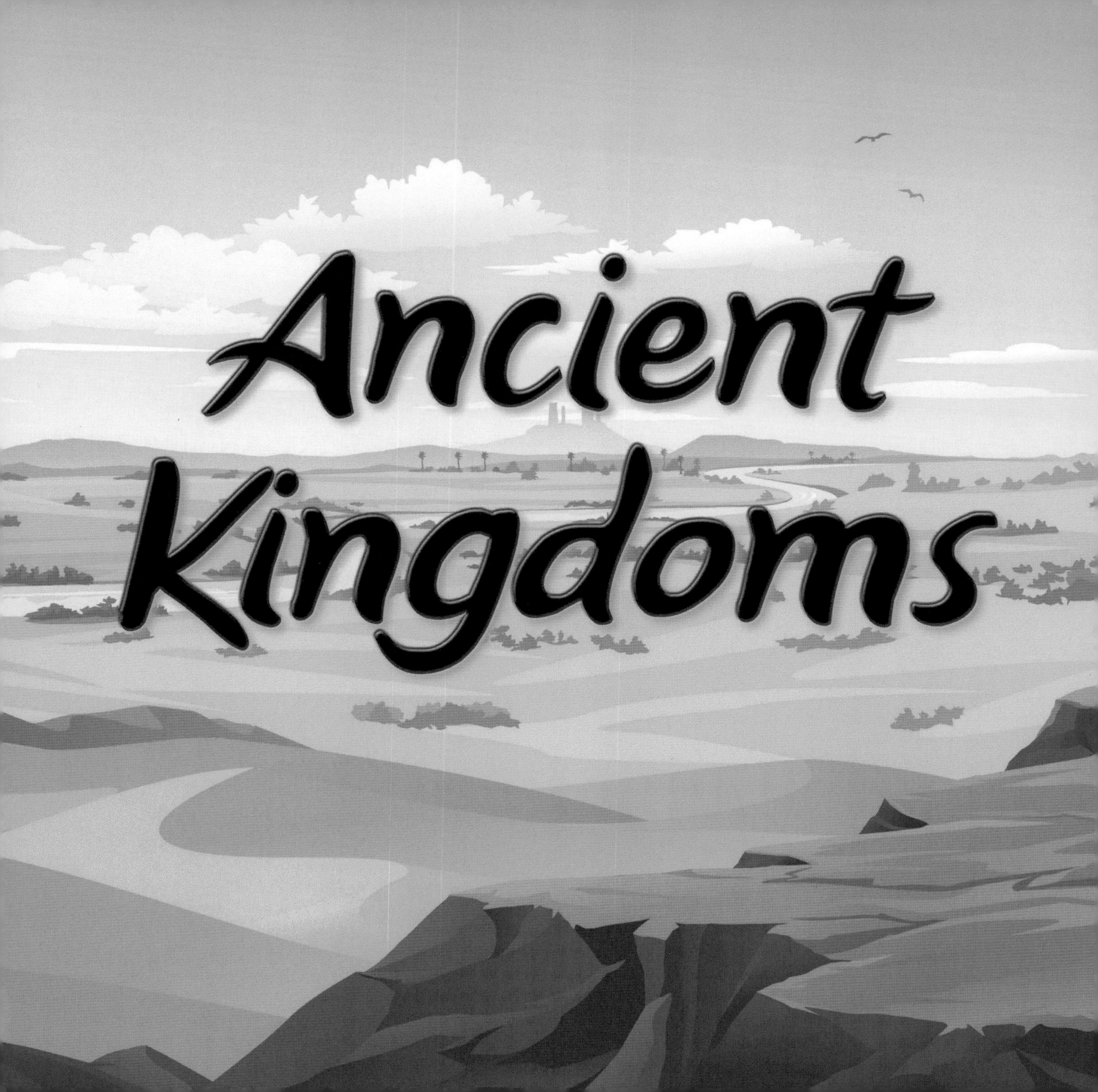

Map of Ancient Egypt

everal ancient kingdoms developed around the Nile River. Egypt and Nubia are two.

Egypt used to be divided into Upper and Lower Egypt. Upper Egypt was south of Lower Egypt. This is because Lower Egypt was downstream of Upper Egypt. A king named Menes is believed to have united the two. One record says that Menes was later killed by a hippopotamus.

King Menes

Nubian pyramids of Meroe in Sudan

Nubia was farther south. Nubia and Egypt fought and ruled over each other throughout history. Eventually, they were both united.

Summary

The Nile River flows from south to north and is the longest river in the world. It is located in northeastern Africa and flows through 10 different countries. The Blue Nile, the White Nile, and the Atabara are the three rivers that feed the Nile.

Lake Victoria is the largest lake in Africa. It is the second largest freshwater lake in the world. Lake Victoria borders Tanzania, Kenya, and Uganda. It is named after Queen Victoria.

The Nile River Basin covers 10 percent of the African continent. It includes the Nile River Delta, which has the most fertile land in Africa.

The climate changes as you go down the Nile. There are tropical humid areas and arid desert areas.

The Nile floods every year, starting in summer. The river is at its highest in mid-September and lowest from March to May. The flood leaves behind black silt which makes it possible to farm in the desert.

The different climates and landscapes around the Nile have different plants and animals. Papyrus was an important plant in ancient Egypt before paper was invented. Nile Crocodiles and hippopotamuses are some of the Nile's most dangerous animals.

Farmers in Egypt and other desert countries along the Nile depend on irrigation. Irrigation probably started in ancient Egypt. Dams are used to store water for irrigation today. Wheat was the most important crop for ancient Egyptians.

Egypt was once split into Upper and Lower Egypt. Egypt was united by King Menes. Nubia and Egypt fought each other for hundreds of years before finally uniting.

Now that you've taken a ride down the Nile, you'll probably want to learn about other rivers! Try reading *The Longest Rivers Lead to the Biggest Oceans – Geography Books for Kids Age 9-12 | Children's Geography Books.*

Visit

www.SpeedyBookStore.com

To view and download free content
on your favorite subject and browse
our catalog of new and exciting
books for readers of all ages.